Chip and Dip

Lovers Cook Book

by

Susan K. Bollin

GOLDEN WEST ☼ PUBLISHERS

Cover photo by Dick Dietrich

Cover design by The Book Studio

Artwork by Jim Tutwiler

Other cook books by Susan K. Bollin:

Salsa Lovers Cook Book

Quick-n-Easy Mexican Recipes

Sedona Cook Book

Library of Congress Cataloging-in-Publication Data

Bollin, Susan
   Chip and Dip Lovers Cook Book / by Susan K. Bollin
      p.   cm.
   Includes index.
   1. Dips (Appetizers)   I. Title. II. Title: Chip and Dip
      Lovers Cook Book
TX740.B615   1993
641.8' 12—dc20
                          93-36756
                          CIP

Printed in the United States of America

ISBN #0-914846-93-0

10th Printing © 1999

Golden West Publishers, Inc.

4113 N. Longview Ave.
Phoenix, AZ 85014, USA

(602) 265-4392

Contents

Vegetable Dips

Bean Dips

Avocado Dips

Meat Dips

Seafood Dips

Mexican Spicy Dips

Salsas

Heated Dips

Dessert Dips

Introduction

As lifestyles have become busier, dips have become a popular mainstay of eating customs. Previously considered a prelude to meals or a cocktail party standard, dips now are an important part of daily eating habits.

Most dips are easy to prepare and require only a few ingredients. They can usually be made in advance and many recipes can be frozen for on-demand eating. There are few more enjoyable foods that are as versatile and easy to prepare as dips. Chips have also become a traditional food. Their popularity has soared in recent years and the diversity in types of chips is unlimited.

Chips, Chips & More Chips

Today's markets offer an endless variety of chips from which to choose. They come in shapes, sizes and flavors undreamed of until recently. There are corn tortilla chips, flour tortilla chips, potato chips, bread chips, bagel chips and even vegetable chips. However, for the purposes of this book, tortilla chips will be the focus of attention.

Tortillas basically are made in two ways—corn and flour. There are many variations of these, such as blue corn and wheat flour. Tortillas are fun and easy to make at home where the assortment of spices to add to them makes experimenting a new taste treat.

The tortilla—the national, basic bread of Mexico—can be shaped in many ways: flat, rolled, basketlike or folded. It can be baked, fried, toasted or microwaved. All of the ingredients, and a few shortcuts, are available in today's markets. The uses and varieties of tortillas know no limits, so experiment and have fun!

Make Your Own Tortillas!
Basic Flour Tortillas

There are many recipes for making flour tortillas at home. Whole wheat flour is widely available along with a variety of white flours.

2 cups FLOUR   **1/4 cup SHORTENING**
1/2 tsp. SALT   **about 1/2 cup WARM WATER**

In a medium bowl, combine flour and salt. With a pastry cutter, or by hand, cut in shortening. Gradually add water, a little at a time, until a soft ball is formed. Shape dough into 12 equal balls and coat with shortening. Cover and let stand for 15 minutes.

On a floured surface, roll each ball into a flat circle. Place each tortilla on an ungreased hot grill, or skillet, and cook over medium-high heat until bubbles form on the top and the bottom is lightly browned. Turn tortilla and cook the other side until tortilla is dry.

Repeat until all tortillas are cooked. Wrap in a warmed kitchen towel until ready to serve. If needed, reheat in microwave on medium power, wrapped in paper towels, or in a 300 degree oven, wrapped in foil.

Makes 12 tortillas.

Most frequently, flour tortillas, whether homemade or purchased commercially, are simply warmed and used in recipes. However, when flour tortillas are deep fried they take on the consistency of french pastry by forming multi-layers of delicate, flaky pastry. This makes them ideal for dessert pastries and for many other uses.

Instant Flour Tortillas

1 pkg. REFRIGERATOR BISCUITS, any type, in dairy case
FLOUR, just enough to lightly flour a small, firm surface

Roll out biscuits on floured surface until very thin. Cook on ungreased grill, or large skillet, over medium-high heat until lightly browned on both sides.

Basic Corn Tortillas

2 cups INSTANT MASA HARINA (available in most markets)
1 cup WATER

Place masa in a medium bowl. Slowly add water and work with hands to make a soft dough. If mix is too dry and crumbly, add more water, a teaspoon at a time. Shape dough into a ball, cover with a damp kitchen towel and let rest for 15 minutes.

Preheat an ungreased grill or large skillet over medium heat.

Divide dough into 12 balls. If using a tortilla press, follow manufacturer's directions for shaping dough. If shaping by hand, place dough between 2 pieces of waxed paper and roll with rolling pin to desired size or about a 6-inch circle. Bake tortillas until lightly browned on both sides.

Makes 12 tortillas.

Tortilla Facts

Flour tortillas can be purchased in a variety of sizes, such as 6, 8, 12 and 15 inch, depending upon their intended use.

Corn tortillas are commercially available in only one size and that is 6 inches in diameter.

- To make **flavored tortillas,** use the following for both flour and corn recipes:

- To make **RED TORTILLAS**, add red chile powder to the dough.

- To make **GREEN TORTILLAS**, add finely diced green chiles to the dough.

    Note: These are especially fun for the holidays!

- To make **SWEET or DESSERT TORTILLAS**, add sugar, cinnamon, powdered sugar or brown sugar to the dough.

- To make **DRUNKEN TORTILLAS**, use half water and half bourbon or tequila when preparing the dough.

Make Your Own Chips!

Chips, both corn and flour, are easy and fun to make at home, using either tortillas from the market or tortillas made at home. If using homemade tortillas, make chips from cooked tortillas.

Traditional Chips

Cut corn tortillas into quarters. Fry, in single layer, in 1 inch deep vegetable oil over medium high heat until crispy. Drain on paper towels and salt to taste.

Ranch Chips

Dip whole corn tortillas in very lightly salted water. While still wet, cut into quarters. Arrange on a cookie sheet, single layered, and bake in a 450 degree preheated oven for approximately 6 minutes, turning chips after 3 minutes.

Note: This method is for corn tortillas only.

Oven Toasted Chips

12 CORN or FLOUR TORTILLAS
3 Tbsp. VEGETABLE OIL

Using a pastry brush, coat one side of each tortilla with oil. Stack the tortillas, oiled side up, in groups of 4 and cut into quarters or more, pizza style. Arrange pieces, single layered, on a baking sheet, oiled side up, and toast in a 350 degree oven for 10-15 minutes or until lightly browned and crispy.

Dips

Creamy Dips

Spinach with Feta Cheese Dip

2 cups SOUR CREAM
1 pkg. (10 1/2 oz.) frozen chopped SPINACH
1/4 lb. FETA CHEESE, cubed
1 GARLIC CLOVE, crushed
1 Tbsp. DILL SEED

Place sour cream in a medium bowl. Cook spinach according to package directions and drain thoroughly. Stir spinach into the sour cream. Add the remaining ingredients, stirring gently.

Makes about 3 cups.

Red Spinach Dip

1 cup SOUR CREAM
1 pkg. (3 oz.) CREAM CHEESE
1 pkg. (10 1/2 oz.) frozen, chopped SPINACH
1 tsp. crushed RED PEPPERS, dried, from jar
1 lg. or 2 med. TOMATOES, peeled, seeded and diced

In a medium bowl, combine sour cream and cream cheese and blend well. Set aside. Cook spinach according to package directions, drain very well and add to sour cream and cheese. Stir in peppers and tomatoes. Serve at room temperature.

Makes about 2 cups.

Sunflower Dip

1 pkg. (8 oz.) CREAM CHEESE
1 cup MONTEREY JACK CHEESE, grated
1/2 cup SUNFLOWER SEEDS

In a medium bowl, combine the cheeses and allow to soften. When soft, mash together with fork. Stir in the seeds. Serve at room temperature.

Makes about 2 cups.

White Asparagus Dip

1 lg. can (15 oz.) WHITE ASPARAGUS TIPS, drained
2 pkgs. (3 oz. each) CREAM CHEESE WITH PIMENTO, softened
1/3 cup SOUR CREAM
1 Tbsp. ONION, grated
1 tsp. LEMON JUICE

Drain asparagus and set aside. In a medium bowl, cream together the cream cheese and sour cream. Add onion and lemon juice. Stir in the asparagus and blend gently. Serve chilled.

Makes about 2 1/2 cups.

Blue Dip

1 pkg. (8 oz.) CREAM CHEESE, softened
1 cup (8 oz.) BLUE CHEESE, crumbled
1/2 cup CREAM
1/2 tsp. TABASCO® SAUCE

In a medium bowl, stir all the ingredients with a fork until completely blended.

Makes about 2 cups.

Double Dip

2 cups COTTAGE CHEESE, creamed
1 can (4 oz.) diced GREEN CHILES
1 Tbsp. ONION, diced
1 1/2 cups LONGHORN or MEDIUM CHEDDAR
**   CHEESE, grated**
1 pkg. (3 oz.) CREAM CHEESE WITH CHIVES, softened
1 tsp. SUGAR
1 tsp. DRY MUSTARD

Combine cottage cheese, chiles and onion in a medium bowl. Stir to blend. Stir in the remaining ingredients. Serve chilled or at room temperature.

Makes about 3 cups.

When doubling a recipe, do not double the seasonings until the recipe is tasted. The original amount may be enough.

Dilled Dip

1 cup SOUR CREAM
1 pkg. (3 oz.) CREAM CHEESE WITH CHIVES
2 tsp. DILL WEED
1 Tbsp. ONION, chopped
1 tsp. cream style HORSERADISH

Combine all ingredients and stir well.

Makes about 1 1/2 cups.

Red Pepper with Chutney Dip

2 Tbsp. OLIVE OIL
1/2 cup ONION, diced
1 lg. or 2 med. RED BELL PEPPER, seeded and diced
1/2 cup CHUTNEY, from jar
3 Tbsp. SHERRY
1 pkg. (8 oz.) CREAM CHEESE, softened

Place olive oil in a medium skillet over medium heat. Sauté onion and bell pepper until limp. Turn off heat, add chutney and sherry and allow to rest for 5 minutes. Stir in cream cheese and blend well. Place dip in a medium serving bowl, cover and refrigerate several hours or overnight.

Makes about 2 cups.

Spinach with Cottage Cheese Dip

1 cup uncreamed COTTAGE CHEESE
1/3 cup MAYONNAISE
1 pkg. (10 1/2 oz.) frozen chopped SPINACH
1/4 cup ONION, grated
2 tsp. dried DILL SEED

Place all ingredients in a blender and process until smooth. Serve well chilled.

Makes about 1 3/4 cups.

Zucchini Dip

1 cup SOUR CREAM
2 pkgs. (3 oz. each) CREAM CHEESE WITH CHIVES
2 cups ZUCCHINI, grated and well drained
1 tsp. dried SWEET BASIL

In a medium bowl, blend sour cream and cream cheese together. Stir in zucchini and basil.

Makes about 3 cups.

Curried Egg Dip

1 cup COTTAGE CHEESE, drained
2 pkgs. (3 oz. each) CREAM CHEESE WITH CHIVES
1 Tbsp. MILK
1 tsp. LEMON JUICE
1/2 tsp. DRY MUSTARD
1/2 tsp. CURRY POWDER
2 EGGS, hard boiled, mashed

Combine all the ingredients in a food processor or blender and process until smooth. Serve chilled.

Makes about 2 cups.

Country Dip

1 pkg. (8 oz.) CREAM CHEESE, softened
3/4 cup MAYONNAISE
1 Tbsp. SUGAR
1/3 cup fresh LIME JUICE
1 Tbsp. freshly grated LIME PEEL
1 Tbsp. Dijon style MUSTARD
1 pkg. (10 1/2 oz.) frozen tiny GREEN PEAS

In a large bowl, beat cream cheese, mayonnaise and sugar together. Add lime juice, lime peel and mustard and stir well. Set aside. Place frozen peas in a colander and run under hot water to separate. Drain peas thoroughly and let cool. When cooled, add to cheese mixture and stir to blend. Serve chilled or at room temperature.

Makes about 2 1/2 cups.

Cold dips, as well as other cold foods, require more concentrated seasoning than do hot dips.

Italian Cheese Dip

1 pkg. (8 oz.) CREAM CHEESE, softened
1 Tbsp. CREAM
1 1/2 cups LONGHORN or MEDIUM CHEDDAR
    CHEESE, grated
1 pkg. (dry) ITALIAN SALAD DRESSING MIX
2 Tbsp. GREEN OLIVES WITH PIMENTOS, chopped

    Place cream cheese in a medium bowl and stir in cream. Add cheese, salad dressing mix and olives and stir to mix. If desired, a 2 ounce jar of diced pimentos can be substituted for the olives.

    Makes about 2 cups.

Spinach Dip

1 cup SOUR CREAM
1 cup MAYONNAISE
1 pkg. (10 oz.) frozen
    SPINACH, chopped,
    thawed and drained

1/2 cup ONION, diced
1 med. TOMATO, diced
1 can (7 oz.) diced
    GREEN CHILES

    Combine all ingredients in a large bowl. Stir well.

    Makes about 3 cups.

Orange Walnut Dip

1 lg. ORANGE, unpeeled, quartered and seeded
1 1/2 cup WALNUTS
2 cups RAISINS
1 cup SALAD DRESSING or MAYONNAISE
1 tsp. ALLSPICE

Place orange sections in a food processor and chop well. Add the remaining ingredients and process until finely chopped and blended. Serve well chilled.

Makes about 3 cups.

Quickie Garlic Dip

3 pkgs. (3 oz. each) CREAM CHEESE WITH
**   CHIVES, softened**
1 Tbsp. CREAM or MILK
2 lg. or 3 sm. GARLIC CLOVES, peeled and crushed

Combine cream cheese and cream or milk and beat well. Stir in garlic.

Makes about 1 cup.

To peel a garlic clove easily, place the clove on a flat surface and place the flat side of a large knife over it. Strike the knife blade sharply against the clove and the skin will slip off. If several cloves are to be peeled at the same time, drop them into boiling water for a few seconds and the skins will easily slip off.

Cucumber Dip

1 pkg. (8 oz.) CREAM CHEESE, softened
1 lg. CUCUMBER, peeled, seeded and diced
1 Tbsp. ONION, grated
1 tsp. RED PEPPER SAUCE

Combine the ingredients in a medium bowl and stir well to blend.

Makes about 1 1/4 cups.

Yellow Dip

1 pkg. (8 oz.) CREAM CHEESE, softened
1/3 cup MAYONNAISE
1 EGG, hard boiled
1 Tbsp. ONION, grated
1/8 tsp. seasoned PEPPER, ground

Soften cream cheese in a medium bowl. Beat in mayonnaise until thoroughly mixed. Mash egg in a small bowl, add onion and pepper and stir well. Add egg mixture to cream cheese mixture and refrigerate for about an hour.

Makes about 1 1/2 cups.

Pimento Dip

3 pkgs. (3 oz. each) **CREAM CHEESE WITH PIMENTOS**,
   softened
1 jar (2 oz.) **PIMENTOS**, diced
1/4 cup **MAYONNAISE**
1/4 cup **PECANS**, finely diced
1/2 tsp. **TABASCO® SAUCE**
1 Tbsp. **BOURBON**

In a medium bowl, combine cream cheese, pimentos and
mayonnaise. Blend very well. Add pecans, Tabasco sauce
and bourbon and stir.

Makes about 1 1/2 cups.

Egg Salad Dip

4 **EGGS**, hard boiled, chopped
2 Tbsp. **SWEET ONION**, grated (if onion is strong,
   reduce amount to 1 Tbsp.)
1 pkg. (3 oz.) **CREAM CHEESE**, softened
1/3 cup **MAYONNAISE**
1/4 tsp. seasoned **SALT**
1/4 tsp. seasoned **PEPPER**
1 tsp. **CURRY POWDER**

Combine ingredients in a large bowl and beat with a
fork until creamy.

Makes about 1 1/2 cups.

Note: This also is delicious as a sandwich spread.

Veggie Special

1 cup SOUR CREAM
1 pkg. dry VEGETABLE SOUP MIX
1 pkg. frozen chopped SPINACH, thawed and well
    drained
1 cup MAYONNAISE
2 Tbsp. ONION, minced

Combine all in a medium bowl and stir until well mixed.
Serve chilled or at room temperature.

Makes about 3 cups.

Dip It Dip

1 pkg. (8 oz.) CREAM CHEESE
1/2 cup BUTTER or MARGARINE
1 Tbsp. MILK
2 Tbsp. ONION, diced
1/2 tsp. CELERY SEED
1 tsp. dried DILL
1 tsp. PARSLEY FLAKES

In a medium bowl, blend cream cheese, butter or margarine and milk. When well blended, add the remaining
ingredients. Serve chilled.

Makes about 2 1/2 cups.

Yogurt Cucumber Dip

2 cups YOGURT, plain or lemon flavored
1 lg. CUCUMBER, peeled, seeded and diced
2 Tbsp. OLIVE OIL
1 tsp. dried DILL SEED
2 GARLIC CLOVES, crushed

Drain yogurt, if necessary, and place in a medium bowl. Add the remaining ingredients and refrigerate until very well chilled.

Makes about 2 1/2 cups.

Celery Dip

1 pkg. (8 oz.) CREAM CHEESE, softened
2 tsp. CELERY SEED
2 tsp. ONION, grated
1 jar (2 oz.) PIMENTOS, diced
1 tsp. WORCESTERSHIRE SAUCE or JALAPEÑO JUICE

Combine the softened cream cheese with the other ingredients and blend thoroughly. Serve at room temperature.

Makes about 1 cup.

Beer Dip

1 pkg. (8 oz.) CREAM CHEESE
1/2 cup BEER
3/4 cup LONGHORN or MEDIUM CHEDDAR
  CHEESE, grated
2 GARLIC CLOVES, crushed
1 Tbsp. SWEET PICKLE RELISH

Soften cream cheese in a medium bowl. Stir in remaining ingredients and stir until well blended.

Makes about 2 cups.

Watercress Dip

1 pkg. (8 oz.) CREAM CHEESE
1 pkg. (3 oz.) CREAM CHEESE WITH CHIVES
1/4 cup SOUR CREAM
1/4 tsp. GARLIC PEPPER
1 tsp. cream style HORSERADISH
1/4 tsp. TABASCO® SAUCE
2 Tbsp. LIME JUICE
1 sm. ONION, chopped
1 lg. or 2 sm. bunches WATERCRESS LEAVES

Place all ingredients in a food processor or blender and blend smooth.

Makes about 2 cups.

Freshly minced or crushed garlic produces the best garlic flavors. Do not substitute garlic salt or other garlic powder if possible.

Black Dip

2 cups LONGHORN CHEESE, grated
1 cup MAYONNAISE (not salad dressing)
1 1/2 cups BLACK OLIVES, diced
6 GREEN ONIONS, chopped
1 Tbsp. PARSLEY FLAKES
1 tsp. CURRY POWDER

Combine all the ingredients in a medium mixing bowl and chill well. Cover and store in the refrigerator.

Makes about 3 cups.

Snappy Dip

4 pkgs. (3 oz. each) CREAM CHEESE WITH PIMENTO
1/2 cup SOUR CREAM
1/2 cup hot SNAPPY TOM® COCKTAIL or other hot
    tomato juice cocktail with chiles

Soften cream cheese in a medium bowl. Stir in sour cream and juice and stir until completely blended. Serve well chilled.

Makes about 1 1/2 cups.

Swiss Dip

3 pkgs. (3 oz. each) CREAM CHEESE WITH CHIVES
1 1/2 cups SWISS CHEESE, finely grated
3 Tbsp. SHERRY

Allow cheeses to soften in a medium bowl. Beat softened cheeses together, stir in sherry. Serve chilled.

Makes about 2 1/2 cups.

Southwestern Dip

1 pt. uncreamed COTTAGE CHEESE
1 can (4 oz.) diced GREEN CHILES, undrained
1/2 cup MAYONNAISE (not salad dressing)
1 med. TOMATO, diced
1/4 cup ONION, diced
2 Tbsp. prepared SALSA

Combine the ingredients in a medium bowl. Serve chilled.

Makes about 2 1/2 cups.

Chile or chili? The word "chile" refers to the chile plant and its pods. The word "chili" refers to a specific dish, such as chili con carne.

Garlic Dip with Capers

1 1/2 cup SOUR CREAM
1 cup cream style COTTAGE CHEESE, drained
1/4 cup CAPERS, drained
2 GARLIC CLOVES, finely minced
1 Tbsp. LIME JUICE

Combine sour cream and cheese in food processor and process until smooth. Place in a medium bowl and add the remaining ingredients. Stir to blend. Chill for 2 or more hours.

Makes about 2 1/2 cups.

Instant Dip

2 cups plain YOGURT
1 pkg. dry ITALIAN SALAD DRESSING MIX

Stir together and chill.

Makes about 2 cups.

Tomato Dip

1 lg. or 2 med. TOMATOES, peeled, seeded and diced
1/4 cup LIME JUICE
1/4 cup GREEN ONIONS, diced
2 cups SOUR CREAM
1 tsp. WORCESTERSHIRE SAUCE

In a large bowl, toss together tomatoes, lime juice and onions. Stir in sour cream and Worcestershire sauce. Chill well.

Makes about 3 cups.

Monterey Dip

1 cup MONTEREY JACK CHEESE, grated
1 jar (2 oz.) diced PIMENTOS, drained
1/3 cup COTTAGE CHEESE
1 Tbsp. MILK
1 GREEN ONION, diced

In a small bowl, combine cheese and pimentos. In another bowl, cream cottage cheese and milk together. Combine the mixtures and add onion. Serve chilled.

Makes about 1 1/3 cups.

Sweet & Sour Onion Dip

3 Tbsp. OLIVE OIL (do not use vegetable oil)
3 lg. SWEET ONIONS, chopped
1 cup SOUR CREAM
1 Tbsp. BASIL VINEGAR

Heat olive oil in a large skillet and add onions. Cook for 12 to 15 minutes over medium heat to caramelize onions. Remove from heat, let cool. Empty sour cream into a medium bowl and stir in vinegar. Add onions and stir to mix.

Makes about 1 1/2 cups.

Blue Beer Dip

2 pkgs. (3 oz. each) CREAM CHEESE, softened
1 1/2 cup BLUE CHEESE, crumbled
1/3 cup BEER
1 1/2 tsp. WORCESTERSHIRE SAUCE

Place all ingredients in food processor and process until smooth.

Makes about 2 cups.

Yogurt with Herbs Dip

2 cups plain YOGURT
1/2 cup CUCUMBER, peeled, seeded and diced
1/4 tsp. GARLIC PEPPER
1 tsp. FINES HERBES®

Blend all together in a small bowl. Cover and refrigerate several hours to allow the flavors to blend.

Makes about 2 cups.

Herbs are fun to grow. They grow well in containers that take up very little space. Fresh herbs add a special touch to recipes.

Party Dip

1 pkg. (8 oz.) CREAM CHEESE, softened
2 cups SHARP CHEDDAR CHEESE, grated
1/4 cup ONION, diced
1/2 cup RED WINE
1 Tbsp. BRANDY

Combine all the ingredients in a large bowl and blend with a hand mixer or food processor. Chill overnight.

Makes 2 1/2 cups.

Creamy Roquefort Dip

1 pkg. (8 oz.) CREAM CHEESE, softened
1/2 cup ROQUEFORT CHEESE, crumbled
2 Tbsp. CREAM
1 tsp. WORCESTERSHIRE SAUCE

Blend all the ingredients until smooth. Serve chilled.

Makes about 1 1/2 cups.

To grate cheese easily, place in the freezer for 15 minutes or so until the cheese hardens. If using a hand-held grater, put it in the freezer with the cheese. This makes the cheese move more easily against the grater.

Sesame Dip

1 cup BLUE CHEESE
1 pkg. (8 oz.) CREAM CHEESE
1 cup SESAME SEEDS
1 can (4 oz.) chopped BLACK OLIVES
1/4 cup BRANDY

Cream blue cheese and cream cheese together until smooth. Stir in seeds, olives and brandy. Serve at room temperature.

Makes about 2 1/2 cups.

Bourbon Cheese Dip

4 cups SHARP CHEDDAR CHEESE, grated
1/3 cup MAYONNAISE
1/2 cup SOUR CREAM
4 Tbsp. BOURBON
1 tsp. RED PEPPER SAUCE
1 cup PECANS, ground

Combine all the ingredients in a large bowl. Beat well to blend. Serve chilled.

Makes about 3 cups.

Chestnut Dip

1 cup SOUR CREAM
3 Tbsp. MAYONNAISE
1 1/2 Tbsp. SOY SAUCE
1 sm. can (3 oz.) WATER CHESTNUTS,
    drained and diced
1 tsp. ground GINGER
1/4 cup fresh CILANTRO LEAVES, chopped

Blend all the ingredients in a medium bowl and chill.

Makes about 1 1/2 cups.

Hot & Cool Dip

2 pkgs. (8 oz. each) CREAM CHEESE, softened
1 lg. CUCUMBER, peeled and seeded
1/4 cup ONION, grated
1/8 cup LEMON or LIME JUICE
1/2 tsp. TABASCO® SAUCE

Place cream cheese in a medium bowl to soften. When soft, stir in the remaining ingredients. Refrigerate until ready to serve. Makes about 2 cups.

Note: To soften cream cheese in a hurry, place in a microwave safe bowl and microwave on high, checking every 30 seconds until desired consistency is obtained.

Ranchero Dip

2 cups SOUR CREAM
1 1/2 cup MAYONNAISE
3 Tbsp. DILL WEED
1 Tbsp. dried CILANTRO LEAVES
1/4 cup RED ONION, minced

Beat sour cream and mayonnaise together with a wire whisk. When thoroughly blended, add the remaining ingredients and stir well.

Makes about 2 1/2 cups.

Double Dill Dip

1 cup SOUR CREAM
1 cup MAYONNAISE
2 Tbsp. DILL SEED, from jar
2 tsp. dried PARSLEY FLAKES
1 tsp. seasoned PEPPER
1/2 tsp. seasoned SALT

In a medium bowl, combine the ingredients and blend well. Serve chilled.

Makes about 2 cups.

Red Radish Dip

3 pkgs. (3 oz. each) CREAM CHEESE WITH CHIVES, softened
1/4 cup MAYONNAISE
3 cups RADISHES, finely diced
1/4 tsp. TABASCO® SAUCE

Combine cream cheese and mayonnaise in a medium bowl. Put radishes through the coarse chopper of a food processor. Stir radishes and Tabasco sauce into cheese mixture.

Makes about 2 cups.

Bright Dip

1 cup SOUR CREAM
1 pkg. SALAD DRESSING MIX, any flavor
1/2 cup CUCUMBER, peeled, seeded and diced
1 jar (2 oz.) PIMENTOS, drained
1/2 cup BELL PEPPER, any color, seeded and diced

Mix the ingredients together and chill for several hours to blend flavors.

Makes about 1 1/2 cups.

Deviled Egg Dip

6 EGGS, hard boiled, mashed
1 can (4 oz.) chopped BLACK OLIVES
3/4 cup MAYONNAISE
1 tsp. CURRY POWDER
1/4 tsp. prepared MUSTARD
1/2 cup PECANS, crushed

Blend all the ingredients together in a medium bowl. Cover and chill for 1 to 2 hours.

Makes about 1 1/3 cups.

Smoky Egg Dip

6 EGGS, hard boiled, mashed
3/4 cup MAYONNAISE
1/3 tsp. DRY MUSTARD
1 tsp. LIQUID SMOKE

In a medium bowl, blend eggs and mayonnaise together. Add mustard and liquid smoke and beat well. Serve chilled.

Makes about 1 1/4 cups.

Before hard boiling eggs, pierce the broad end of each egg with a needle. This keeps the shells from cracking during boiling.

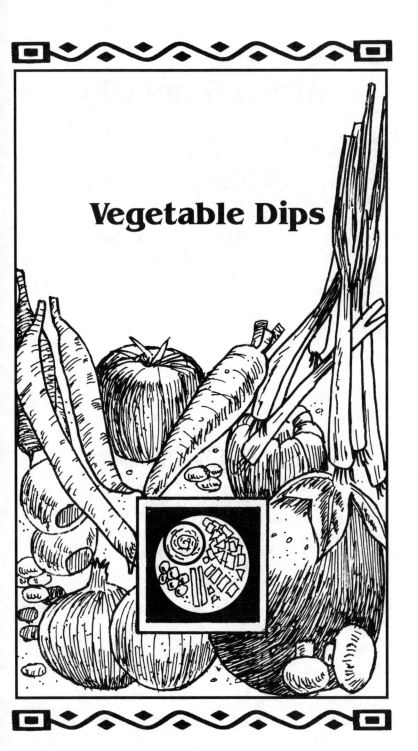

Vegetable Dips

Green Bean Dip

2 pkgs. (10 1/2 oz. each) frozen cut GREEN BEANS
3 Tbsp. BUTTER or MARGARINE
1 med. ONION, chopped
1/2 cup ITALIAN FLAVORED BREAD CRUMBS
3 EGGS, hard boiled, chopped
1 tsp. seasoned PEPPER

Cook beans according to package directions, omitting salt. Drain well and set aside. Melt butter or margarine in a small skillet and sauté onions until limp and lightly browned. Place beans, onions and remaining ingredients in food processor and process until almost smooth. Place in a medium bowl and serve chilled.

Makes about 3 cups.

Black Olive Dip

1 can (4 1/2 oz.) sliced or diced BLACK OLIVES
1 sm. jar (6 oz.) marinated ARTICHOKE HEARTS,
**   drained and diced**
1 pkg. (3 oz.) CREAM CHEESE WITH CHIVES, softened
2 tsp. dried SWEET BASIL

In a small bowl, combine olives and artichoke hearts. With a fork, stir in softened cream cheese and basil. Serve chilled.

Makes about 1 cup.

Cauliflower Dip

4 Tbsp. BUTTER or MARGARINE
2 stalks CELERY, chopped
1/2 cup ONION, diced
1 can (4 oz.) MUSHROOMS, drained and diced
1 pkg. (8 oz.) CREAM CHEESE
1 can (10 1/2 oz.) CREAM OF MUSHROOM SOUP,
     undiluted
1 pkg. (10 1/2 oz.) frozen chopped CAULIFLOWER
1/2 tsp. TABASCO® SAUCE

Melt butter or margarine in a large skillet. Sauté celery, onion and mushrooms in butter until limp. Reduce heat to low, stir in cream cheese and soup. Cook cauliflower according to package directions. Drain well, chop fine and add to skillet. Stir in Tabasco sauce. Serve warm.

Makes about 4 cups.

Mushroom Supreme Dip

3 Tbsp. OLIVE OIL
1 lb. fresh MUSHROOMS, washed and chopped
1 sm. RED ONION, chopped
1/4 tsp. seasoned PEPPER or PEPPER MÉLANGE
1 tsp. TARRAGON VINEGAR
1 Tbsp. SHERRY
1 pkg. (3 oz.) CREAM CHEESE WITH CHIVES, softened

Place oil in a large skillet over medium-high heat. Add mushrooms and onion and cook until all of the moisture from the mushrooms is evaporated, about 15 minutes. Remove from heat and stir in the remaining ingredients. Bring to room temperature, cover and refrigerate several hours or overnight.

Makes about 2 cups.

Mushroom Dip

3 Tbsp. BUTTER or MARGARINE
1 lb. fresh MUSHROOMS, chopped
2 Tbsp. FLOUR
3/4 cup WHIPPING CREAM
1/2 tsp. ground NUTMEG

Melt butter in a large skillet. Sauté mushrooms until reduced to one-half the original amount. Stir in flour, slowly add cream and nutmeg. Cook over low heat, stirring frequently, until mixture is thickened to dipping consistency. Serve warm.

Makes about 1 1/2 cups.

Super Veggie Dip

1 cup SOUR CREAM
1/4 cup ONION, diced
1 can (8 oz.) MEXICORN®, drained
1 pkg. (10 1/2 oz.) frozen TINY PEAS, blanched under
    hot water
1 can (4 oz.) diced GREEN CHILES
1/4 tsp. TABASCO® SAUCE

Combine all ingredients in a medium bowl. Serve chilled.

Makes about 3 cups.

Eggplant Dip

1 med. EGGPLANT, cooked
1/3 cup OLIVE OIL
1 sm. ONION, diced
1/4 cup TOMATO PASTE
1 GARLIC CLOVE, crushed
1 Tbsp. LEMON JUICE

Bake the eggplant in a 350 degree oven until tender. Cool, peel and dice. Set aside. Heat olive oil in a medium skillet and sauté onions until limp. Add eggplant and the remaining ingredients and cook about 20 minutes over medium heat. Remove from heat, let cool and pureé in a food processor or blender. Serve at room temperature.

Makes about 3 cups.

Bean Dips

Kidney Bean Dip

1 can (15 oz.) KIDNEY BEANS, drained and rinsed
1 tsp. CHILI POWDER
1/4 tsp. ground CUMIN
1 Tbsp. WHITE WINE VINEGAR
1 Tbsp. ONION, chopped

Combine all the ingredients in a food processor and process until smooth. Serve at room temperature.

Makes about 2 cups.

Olé Dip

1 can (15 oz.) REFRIED BEANS
3/4 cup BEER
1 cup PROVOLONE CHEESE, shredded
3 Tbsp. BUTTER or MARGARINE
1 Tbsp. CHILI POWDER

Combine all the ingredients in a large skillet and sauté over low heat, stirring frequently, until the cheese melts. Serve warm.

Makes about 2 cups.

Rancho Dip

1 lg. can (15 oz.) RANCH STYLE BEANS
1 cup LONGHORN CHEESE, grated
2 fresh JALAPEÑO CHILES, seeded and diced
1 pkg. (3 oz.) CREAM CHEESE WITH CHIVES, softened

Drain beans and place in food processor and process until smooth. Stir in remaining ingredients and chill to blend flavors. Serve warm or chilled.

Makes about 2 1/4 cups.

Mi Amigo Dip

1 can (15 oz.) REFRIED BEANS
2 cups SOUR CREAM
1 cup SALSA

Combine the ingredients in a medium bowl. Serve warm or chilled.

Makes about 4 cups.

Delicioso Dip

2 cups BEANS, black or pinto, mashed
1 can (7 oz.) diced GREEN CHILES
1 GARLIC CLOVE, crushed
1 tsp. WORCESTERSHIRE SAUCE

In a large bowl, mash beans. Add chiles, garlic and Worcestershire sauce and stir well. Serve at room temperature.

Makes about 2 1/2 cups.

Adobe Dip

1 pt. SOUR CREAM
2 cans (7 oz. each) prepared MEXICAN BEAN DIP

Combine and stir well.

Makes about 3 3/4 cups.

Note: This also makes a quick topping for tostadas.

Bean & Bacon Dip

1 can (10 1/2 oz.) BEAN WITH BACON SOUP
1/4 cup ONION, diced
2 Tbsp. BELL PEPPER, diced
1/4 cup CHILI SAUCE
1/4 tsp. TABASCO® SAUCE

Combine all the ingredients in a food processor or blender and process until smooth. Serve at room temperature.

Makes about 1 1/2 cups.

Beans, called "frijoles" in Spanish, have hundreds of varieties. Two of the most popular in this country are pinto beans and black beans.

Creamy Bean Dip

3 pkgs. (3 oz. each) CREAM CHEESE WITH CHIVES
1 can (10 1/2 oz.) BLACK BEAN SOUP
1 GARLIC CLOVE, peeled and crushed
1/2 tsp. TABASCO® SAUCE

Place cream cheese in a large bowl. Beat until smooth with electric mixer. Beat in soup, garlic and Tabasco. Beat only until smooth, do not overbeat. Serve well chilled.

Makes about 2 cups.

Blanco Bean Dip

1 can (15 or 16 oz.) WHITE BEANS, rinsed and drained
1 Tbsp. LIME or LEMON JUICE
1 GARLIC CLOVE, crushed
1 tsp. OLIVE OIL
1/4 tsp. ground CUMIN
1/4 tsp. dried OREGANO

Place all ingredients in a blender or food processor and blend until smooth. Transfer to a medium serving bowl and chill for about one hour. This can be made a day ahead, covered and refrigerated.

Makes about 1 1/4 cups.

Bueno Bean Dip

1 can (16 oz.) REFRIED BEANS or, 1 can (16 oz.)
    REFRIED BEANS WITH JALAPEÑOS
1 lb. LONGHORN or MEDIUM CHEDDAR CHEESE,
    grated
1 sm. ONION, diced
1 GARLIC CLOVE, crushed

Combine all ingredients in a medium saucepan and cook over low heat until the cheese is melted. Serve warm.

Makes about 4 cups.

S. O. B. Dip
(Same Old Beans)

1 can (15 oz.) PINTO BEANS, drained and rinsed
2 Tbsp. PICKLED JALAPEÑO CHILES, from jar
1 tsp. pickling JUICE, from jar
1 Tbsp. SWEET ONION, chopped
1/8 tsp. ground CUMIN
2 Tbsp. fresh CILANTRO, chopped

Place all ingredients except the cilantro in a food processor or blender. Blend until smooth. Place in a small serving bowl and top with chopped cilantro sprinkled on top.

Makes about 1 cup.

El Dorado Bean Dip

1 can (16 oz.) REFRIED BEANS
1 can (4 oz.) diced GREEN CHILES, drained
1/4 cup MAYONNAISE
1 GARLIC CLOVE, crushed

Combine the ingredients in a medium bowl and refrigerate until chilled.

Makes about 2 cups.

Sonoran Bean Dip

1 can (16 oz.) REFRIED BEANS
1/3 cup ENCHILADA SAUCE
1 cup SOUR CREAM

Combine all ingredients in a food processor or blender. Blend until smooth.

Makes about 3 cups.

Señorita Bean Dip

1 can (15 oz.) REFRIED BEANS
1/4 cup ONIONS, diced
1/4 cup SALSA
1/2 cup LONGHORN or MEDIUM CHEDDAR
    CHEESE, grated

In a medium skillet, combine the refried beans and onions. Cook over medium low heat until onions are limp and well blended with the beans. Add salsa and cheese and stir until cheese melts. Serve warm or at room temperature.

Makes about 2 generous cups.

Avocado Dips

Guacamole

Guacamole, once only familiar to the southwestern United States, has become a national favorite. There are endless versions of this delicious dip. These are my favorites.

2 lg. AVOCADOS, mashed
1 sm. ONION, diced
1 lg. or 2 sm. TOMATOES, chopped
1 can (7 oz.) diced GREEN CHILES
1 GARLIC CLOVE, crushed
1 Tbsp. LIME JUICE

Mash avocados in a medium bowl. Add the remaining ingredients and stir well. Serve at once.

Makes about 2 cups.

Guacamole con Tocino

2 AVOCADOS, mashed
1/2 lb. BACON (tocino), crisply cooked, crumbled
1 tsp. LIME JUICE
2 Tbsp. ONION, diced
4 Tbsp. SOUR CREAM

Combine all in a medium bowl. Serve chilled.

Makes 2 cups.

Quick Dip Guacamole

If guacamole is not to be served at once, leave the avocado pit in the dip until serving time to help prevent darkening. Lemon or lime juice also helps prevent avocados from turning dark.

2 lg. AVOCADOS, mashed
1/2 cup SALSA
1 tsp. LEMON or LIME JUICE

Combine the ingredients in a small bowl.

Makes about 1 cup.

Amazing Avocado Dip

Guacamole is properly pronounced "wok-a-mole-ee."
The beginning "g" is silent.

2 lg. or 3 med. AVOCADOS, mashed
2 pkg. (3 oz. each) CREAM CHEESE WITH PIMENTOS
1 can (4 oz.) diced GREEN CHILES or 2 Tbsp.
JALAPEÑO, seeded and diced
1 Tbsp. ONION, diced
1 Tbsp. LEMON or LIME JUICE

Stir avocados and cream cheese together in a medium bowl until completely blended. Add the chiles, onion and juice and cream together.

Makes about 2 cups.

Señor Verde Dip

3 lg. or 4 med. AVOCADOS, peeled, seeded and mashed
1/2 cup fresh CILANTRO, chopped
2 Tbsp. ONION, grated
2 Tbsp. LIME JUICE
1/4 cup SALSA

Place avocados in a medium bowl and mash well with a fork. Add the remaining ingredients and stir.

Makes about 1 1/2 cups.

Onions are one of the most popular vegetables used in dips. Not only do onions come in many varieties, but other members of the onion family are also used extensively in dip recipes. Some of these are garlic, chives, leeks, green onions (also called scallions) and shallots.

Meat Dips

Italian Sausage Dip

1 pkg. (8 oz.) CREAM CHEESE, softened
1 cup SOUR CREAM
1 lb. bulk ITALIAN SAUSAGE, mild or hot,
    according to taste
1/2 cup ONION, diced

In a medium bowl, beat cream cheese and sour cream together with a wire whisk. Set aside. In a medium skillet, sauté sausage until thoroughly cooked, drain very well and cool. Add cooled sausage to cheese mixture, stir in onions. Serve warm.

Makes about 2 1/2 cups.

Chorizo Dip

2 pkgs. (8 oz. each) CREAM CHEESE, softened
1/2 cup MAYONNAISE
1/2 lb. cooked CHORIZO, drained and crumbled

Beat cream cheese and mayonnaise together. Stir in chorizo. Serve at room temperature.

Makes about 3 cups.

Note: To yield 1/2 cup cooked chorizo will require 1 pound of uncooked sausage.

Fiery Beef Dip

1 pkg. (8 oz.) CREAM CHEESE, softened
1/2 cup SOUR CREAM
1 cup BEEF, cooked medium rare, diced
1/2 cup ONION, diced
1 tsp. TABASCO® SAUCE

Blend the cream cheese and sour cream together until smooth. Stir in the beef, onion and Tabasco. Serve warm or chilled.

Makes about 2 cups.

Honey Ham Dip

1 pkg. (8 oz.) CREAM CHEESE, softened
2 cans (4 1/2 oz. each) DEVILED HAM
1 sm. can (4 oz.) crushed PINEAPPLE, well drained
1 Tbsp. HONEY

Blend the ingredients together in a medium bowl and chill.

Makes about 2 cups.

Sauerkraut Dip

1 cup SOUR CREAM
1/3 cup MAYONNAISE
1 can (15 oz.) SAUERKRAUT, finely diced
1 1/2 cups cooked HAM, chopped
1/2 cup ITALIAN FLAVORED BREAD CRUMBS
1 cup SHARP CHEDDAR CHEESE, grated

In a large bowl, blend sour cream and mayonnaise together. Add the remaining ingredients and stir well to mix thoroughly. Serve chilled.

Makes about 3 cups.

Bacon Dip with Almonds

3/4 cup MAYONNAISE
4 strips BACON, fried crisp and crumbled
1 cup LONGHORN or MEDIUM CHEDDAR CHEESE,
**   grated**
1/2 cup ALMONDS, minced

Stir the ingredients together well to make a dipping consistency.

Makes about 2 cups.

Watercress & Bean Dip

1 pkg. (8 oz.) CREAM CHEESE, softened
1 Tbsp. CREAM
1 tsp. HORSERADISH
1/2 lb. BACON, fried crisp and crumbled
1 bunch WATERCRESS, chopped

Place cream cheese in a medium bowl and blend in cream and horseradish. Add bacon and watercress and stir well.

Makes about 2 cups.

Creamy Beef Dip

3 pkgs. (3 oz. each) CREAM CHEESE WITH
   CHIVES, softened
1/4 cup SOUR CREAM
2 Tbsp. MAYONNAISE
3 Tbsp. BELL PEPPER, diced
1 jar (2 1/2 oz.) DRIED CHIPPED BEEF
1/4 tsp. freshly ground PEPPER

In a medium bowl, stir all the ingredients together. Serve at room temperature.

Makes about 1 3/4 cups.

Hamburger Cheese Dip

*This is a great way to use up small amounts
of leftover cooked hamburger.*

1 cup cooked HAMBURGER
1 sm. ONION, diced
2 cups MEDIUM CHEDDAR CHEESE, grated
1 can (15 oz.) CHILI without beans
1 can (10 1/2 oz.) TOMATOES AND GREEN
    CHILES, drained and chopped

Combine all the ingredients in a medium saucepan and
heat until cheese is almost melted. Serve warm.

Makes about 4 1/2 cups.

**Archaeologists believe that corn began as
a wild grass in Mexico over 50,000 years ago.
Around 4000 B.C., corn was a cultivated crop
and a mainstay of the diet of the Indians of Mexico.**

Red Devil Dip

1 pkg. (8 oz.) CREAM CHEESE, softened
1 can (10 1/2 oz.) TOMATO SOUP
2 cans (4 1/2 oz.) DEVILED HAM
1/2 cup CUCUMBER, peeled, seeded and diced

Combine all the ingredients in a blender or beat together with an electric mixer and blend thoroughly. Serve
chilled.

Makes about 2 1/2 cups.

Bacon Dip

1 pkg. (8 oz.) CREAM CHEESE, softened
8 slices BACON, fried crisp and crumbled
1 tsp. CURRY POWDER

Blend the ingredients together in a small bowl. Serve at room temperature.

Makes 1 1/2 cups.

Ham & Eggs Dip

1 can (3 1/2 oz.) DEVILED HAM
2 EGGS, hard boiled, mashed
YOGURT, plain

In a small bowl, combine ham and eggs. Add enough yogurt to make a dipping consistency.

Makes about 3/4 cup.

Leftover Paté

2 cups leftover cooked MEAT, such as beef, ham
    or chicken
1 Tbsp. melted BUTTER or MARGARINE
1 cup MUSHROOMS, sliced
1/8 tsp. seasoned PEPPER
1/4 cup cream style SHERRY

Cut meat into small pieces and place in a food processor. Process until fairly smooth, add remaining ingredients and continue processing until mixture reaches a smooth consistency. Serve at room temperature.

Makes about 2 1/2 cups.

Liver Paté

4 Tbsp. BUTTER
2 cups (about 1 lb.) fresh
    CHICKEN LIVERS
2 cups fresh MUSHROOMS,
    diced
3 GARLIC CLOVES, crushed

1/2 cup ONION, diced
1/2 tsp. dried THYME
    LEAVES
1/2 tsp. dry MUSTARD
1/2 tsp. ground NUTMEG
1/3 cup SHERRY

Melt butter in a large skillet over medium heat. Use a splatter shield to prevent messy splattering. Add livers, mushrooms, garlic and onion and sauté about 15 minutes or until livers are nicely browned. Do not overcook them as this makes them tough. Add the remaining ingredients and cook over medium-low heat for about 5 minutes. Remove from heat, let cool. Process in a food processor or blender until mixture is smooth. Place in a medium bowl, cover and refrigerate several hours or overnight to blend flavors.

Makes about 2 cups.

Chicken Dip

1 1/2 - 2 cups CHICKEN, very finely diced
1/3 cup MAYONNAISE
1 Tbsp. SWEET or DILL PICKLE RELISH
1 Tbsp. ONION, chopped

Combine the ingredients in a medium bowl and chill.

Makes about 1 1/2 cups.

Corned Beef Dip

2 cans (12 oz. each) CORNED BEEF
3/4 cup MAYONNAISE
1/2 cup ONION, diced
1 tsp. DRY MUSTARD
2 Tbsp. SHERRY or 1 Tbsp. BRANDY

In a large bowl, separate corned beef with a fork until shredded into small pieces. Stir in the remaining ingredients and blend well.

Makes about 3 3/4 cups.

Here Today, Gone to Maui

3 cups HAM, finely diced or ground in a food processor
1 can (8 oz.) crushed PINEAPPLE, thoroughly drained
1/3 cup MAYONNAISE
1 Tbsp. prepared MUSTARD WITH HORSERADISH
　　or other prepared mustards, such as raspberry
　　mustard, if desired

In a large bowl, combine the ingredients. Serve well chilled.

Makes about 4 cups.

Chipped Beef Dip

3 pkgs. (3 oz. each) CREAM CHEESE WITH CHIVES
1 GARLIC CLOVE, crushed
1 can (4 oz.) diced GREEN CHILES, drained
1/2 jar CHIPPED BEEF, diced

Soften cream cheese in a medium bowl. When soft, add the remaining ingredients and stir well. Refrigerate for 2 hours.

Makes about 2 1/2 cups.

Hot Chile Cheese Dip

1 pkg. (8 oz.) CREAM CHEESE
2 Tbsp. MILK
1/2 cup SOUR CREAM
1 jar (2 1/2 oz.) DRIED BEEF, finely diced
1 can (4 oz.) diced GREEN CHILES, drained
3 Tbsp. ONION, grated
freshly ground PEPPER, to taste

In a medium bowl, blend cream cheese, milk and sour cream until smooth. Stir in the remaining ingredients and blend well. Place mixture in a shallow pie pan and bake in a 350 degree oven for 20 minutes. Serve warm.

Makes about 3 cups.

Hammy Ham Dip

3 pkgs. (3 oz. each) CREAM CHEESE WITH PIMENTOS
1/3 cup MAYONNAISE (not salad dressing)
2 cans (2 1/4 oz. each) DEVILED HAM
1/2 tsp. WORCESTERSHIRE SAUCE

Soften cream cheese in a medium bowl. When softened, stir in mayonnaise and beat well. Add ham and Worcestershire sauce and stir until completely blended.

Makes about 2 cups.

Spicy Ham Dip

2 pkgs. (3 oz. each) CREAM CHEESE WITH PIMENTOS
1 pkg. (8 oz.) CREAM CHEESE
2 cans (4 1/2 oz. each) DEVILED HAM
2 tsp. ONION, grated
1/3 cup SOUR CREAM
1/3 cup CHILI SAUCE

Soften cream cheeses in a medium bowl. Blend in the remaining ingredients and stir to mix completely.

Makes about 2 cups.

Patio Paté

1 pkg. (3 oz.) CREAM CHEESE, softened
1/4 lb. BRAUNSWEIGER
1/4 cup WHIPPING CREAM
1/4 cup ground NUTMEG
1/4 cup MUSHROOMS, diced

Combine all ingredients in a medium bowl. Let stand at room temperature for 1/2 hour before serving.

Makes about 1 cup.

Seafood Dips

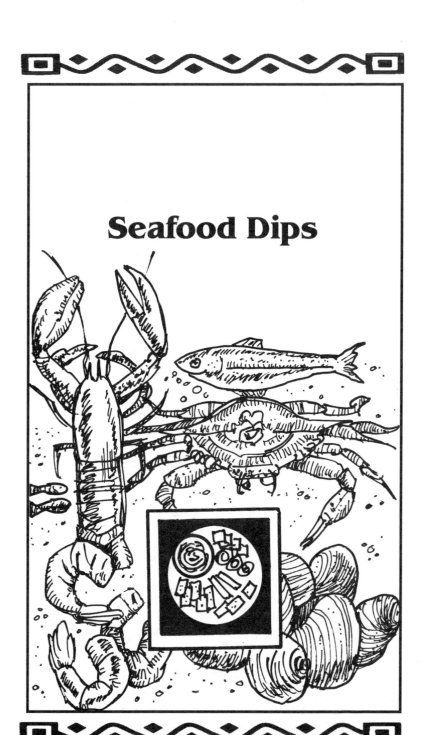

English Shrimp Dip

4 oz. (1/2 block) CREAM CHEESE, softened
1 jar (5 oz.) OLD ENGLISH® CHEDDAR CHEESE
  SPREAD
1 tsp. GARLIC SALT
1 can (4 1/2 oz.) COCKTAIL SHRIMP, drained
  and washed
CREAM, enough to make a dipping consistency,
  about 2 Tbsp.

In a medium bowl, blend cream cheese and cheddar cheese together. Add remaining ingredients and stir well. Add cream as needed.

Makes about 1 1/2 cups.

Tequila Shrimp Dip

2 pkg. (3 oz. each) CREAM CHEESE WITH CHIVES
1 lg. or 2 med. AVOCADOS, mashed
1 tsp. LEMON JUICE
2 Tbsp. TEQUILA
6 lg. SHRIMP, cooked and diced

In a medium bowl, beat cream cheese and avocados together until creamy. Stir in lime juice and tequila. Fold in shrimp.

Makes about 1 1/2 cups.

Sweet Tuna Dip

1 can (6 1/2 oz.) TUNA, drained and flaked
3 EGGS, hard boiled, diced
1 Tbsp. SWEET PICKLE RELISH
1/8 tsp. seasoned PEPPER
1/2 cup MAYONNAISE

Combine the ingredients in a medium bowl and blend well. Chill well.

Makes about 1 1/4 cups.

Easy Clam Dip

1 can (10 1/2 oz.) condensed NEW ENGLAND
**   CLAM CHOWDER, undiluted**
1 sm. can (4 1/2 oz.) minced CLAMS, drained
2 cups MEDIUM CHEDDAR CHEESE, grated
2 Tbsp. FLOUR
1/2 tsp. TABASCO® or other red hot sauce

Heat chowder in a medium saucepan. In a medium bowl, toss cheese with flour to coat. Add slowly to chowder until all cheese is added. Stir in clams and sauce. Heat until cheese melts.

Makes about 2 cups.

Smoked Swordfish Dip

1 1/2 lbs. SMOKED SWORDFISH (or other
    smoked fish to taste)
1 cup MAYONNAISE
1 pkg. (3 oz.) CREAM CHEESE WITH CHIVES
1 Tbsp. ONION, diced
1 tsp. WORCESTERSHIRE SAUCE

Flake fish in a large bowl. Stir in remaining ingredients and blend well. Chill for several hours or overnight.

Makes about 3 cups.

Herring in Sour Cream Dip

1 lg. jar HERRING IN WINE, drained and finely minced
2 cups SOUR CREAM
1 lg. red ONION, sliced very thin

Empty herring into colander to drain well. Cut into small bite-sized pieces and place in a medium bowl. Add sour cream and onions and stir well. Cover and refrigerate for at least 24 hours.

Makes about 3 cups.

Red Anchovy Dip

3 pkgs. (3 oz. each) CREAM CHEESE WITH CHIVES,
   softened
1/3 cup FRENCH SALAD DRESSING
1 Tbsp. CATSUP
2 Tbsp. ANCHOVY PASTE

Combine all the ingredients and blend until smooth. Serve at room temperature.

Makes about 1 1/2 cups.

Easy Caviar Dip

1 pkg. (8 oz.) CREAM CHEESE, softened
1 sm. jar RED or BLACK CAVIAR, to taste

Blend well. Serve at room temperature.

Makes about 1 1/4 cups.

Chinese Crab Dip

1 cup SOUR CREAM
1/2 lb. CRABMEAT, flaked with cartilage removed
1 tsp. CURRY POWDER
1/2 tsp. ONION, grated

Stir all together.

Makes about 1 1/2 cups.

Sardine Dip

1 pkg. (3 oz.) CREAM CHEESE WITH CHIVES, softened
1 Tbsp. MAYONNAISE
2 EGGS, hard boiled, diced
1 Tbsp. LEMON JUICE
2 cans (5 oz. each) SARDINES, packed in oil, drained
freshly ground PEPPER, to taste

Blend the softened cheese and mayonnaise together in a medium bowl. Add remaining ingredients and stir well.

Makes about 1 1/4 cups.

Lobster Dip

1 pkg. (10 1/2 oz.) frozen chopped SPINACH
6 GREEN ONIONS, diced
6 Tbsp. BUTTER or MARGARINE
2 cups cooked LOBSTER, chopped
1/3 cup freshly grated PARMESAN CHEESE

Cook spinach according to package directions and drain very well. Set aside. Place onions and butter in a small skillet and sauté until lightly browned. In a large bowl, combine spinach, onions, lobster and cheese. Microwave on high for 1 to 2 minutes until warm. Serve at once or keep warm in a fondue or crockpot.

Makes about 2 cups.

Sour Cream Quickie Dips

1 pt. (2 cups) SOUR CREAM

Add ONE of the following:
1 cup CLAMS, drained and minced
1 pkg. dry VEGETABLE or ONION SOUP MIX
1 sm. jar CAVIAR

Stir well, cover and refrigerate until ready to serve.

Makes about 2 - 2 1/2 cups.

Cheese & Capers Dip

1 pkg. (8 oz.) CREAM CHEESE
1/4 cup MAYONNAISE
3 ANCHOVIES, diced
1 1/2 tsp. CAPERS
4 GREEN ONIONS, minced
1/8 tsp. seasoned PEPPER, finely ground

Place cream cheese in a medium bowl and allow to soften. Stir in mayonnaise and beat together. Add the remaining ingredients and stir to combine. Cover and refrigerate for several hours.

Makes about 1 1/2 cups.

Tuna & Bean Dip

3 Tbsp. COTTAGE CHEESE
1 Tbsp. MAYONNAISE
1/2 cup ONION, minced
1 sm. can (6 1/2 oz.) TUNA, drained and flaked
1 cup BLACK BEANS (or other beans of choice)
1 Tbsp. dried SWEET BASIL LEAVES
1 Tbsp. LEMON or LIME JUICE

In a large bowl, stir cottage cheese and mayonnaise together until thoroughly blended. Add remaining ingredients and mix. Cover and chill until ready to serve.

Makes about 2 cups.

Smoky Salmon Dip

1 can (15 oz.) SALMON, drained and flaked
1 pkg. (8 oz.) CREAM CHEESE, softened
1 Tbsp. LEMON JUICE
1 tsp. WORCESTERSHIRE SAUCE
1/2 tsp. LIQUID SMOKE (or slightly more, to taste)

Empty drained salmon into a large bowl. Pick through the salmon to remove any bone or cartilage fragments. Add softened cream cheese and blend thoroughly. Add the remaining ingredients and blend.

Makes about 3 cups.

Note: Use either red or pink salmon according to taste. If using pink salmon, a few drops of red food coloring will brighten the appearance of the dip.

Anchovy Salsa Dip

1 pkg. (8 oz.) CREAM CHEESE, softened
6 ANCHOVY FILLETS, mashed
1 GARLIC CLOVE, crushed
1 1/2 Tbsp. diced GREEN CHILES
1/2 cup OLIVE OIL
3 Tbsp. PARSLEY, fresh or dried
LEMON JUICE to taste, not more than 3 Tbsp.

Place cream cheese in a large bowl to soften. When softened, add remaining ingredients and blend well.

Makes about 1 1/2 cups.

Cream Cheese
with Smoked Oysters

1 pkg. (8 oz.) CREAM CHEESE
1 cup MAYONNAISE (not salad dressing)
1/2 tsp. TABASCO® or other hot sauce
1 Tbsp. LEMON JUICE
1 can (3-4 oz.) SMOKED OYSTERS or SMOKED CLAMS,
    drained if necessary

Blend cream cheese and mayonnaise together. Stir in hot sauce and lemon juice. If desired, dice the oysters or clams and add to mixture. Stir to combine well.

Makes about 3 1/2 cups.

Salmon Dip

1 pkg. (8 oz.) CREAM CHEESE, softened
1/4 cup MILK or CREAM
1 Tbsp. LIME JUICE
1/8 tsp. WORCESTERSHIRE SAUCE
1 cup canned SALMON, flaked

Combine all the ingredients and blend very well. Shape into a ball and refrigerate for 1-2 hours.

Makes about 2 cups.

Shredded Crab Dip

1 cup SOUR CREAM
1 cup COTTAGE CHEESE, drained if necessary
1/2 lb. CRABMEAT, shredded and any cartilage removed
1 Tbsp. LEMON JUICE
1/2 tsp. seasoned PEPPER
1/4 tsp. seasoned SALT

Combine all the ingredients in a medium bowl and chill.

Makes about 3 cups.

Baja Shrimp Dip

1 pkg. (8 oz.) CREAM CHEESE
1 can (4-5 oz.) SHRIMP
1 Tbsp. HORSERADISH
1 tsp. ONION, diced
3 Tbsp. grated CUCUMBER, peeled and seeded

Soften cream cheese in a medium bowl. Stir in the remaining ingredients and blend well. Serve chilled.

Makes about 2 1/2 cups.

Coastal Dip

1 pkg. (8 oz.) CREAM CHEESE
1 cup prepared CHILI SAUCE
8 oz. CRABMEAT, flaked
1 tsp. ONION SALT

Soften the cream cheese in a medium bowl. Stir in the remaining ingredients. Serve at room temperature.

Makes about 2 cups.

Spicy Shrimp Dip

6 lg. cooked SHRIMP, diced
1 pkg. (8 oz.) CREAM CHEESE
1/2 cup CHILI SAUCE
1 tsp. HORSERADISH
1/2 tsp. CELERY SEED

Dice shrimp and set aside. In a medium bowl, stir cream cheese to soften. Add chili sauce, horseradish and celery seed. Mix well. Stir in shrimp.

Makes about 1 1/2 cups.

Note: Do not use canned miniature shrimp (also called bay shrimp) in this recipe.

Shrimp Cocktail Dip

2 cups bottled CHILI SAUCE (not catsup)
2 tsp. HORSERADISH, cream style
2 tsp. LIME JUICE
1/4 cup fresh CILANTRO, finely diced

Combine the ingredients in a medium bowl. Cover and chill at least one hour or longer to blend the flavors. Serve cold.

Makes about 2 1/4 cups.

Mexican Spicy Dips

Grace's Jalapeño Dip

3 jars (5 oz. each) KRAFT® BACON CHEESE SPREAD
2 cans (10 1/2 oz. each) CREAM OF MUSHROOM SOUP
1 sm. ONION, chopped
4 fresh JALAPEÑO CHILES, seeded and diced
3 lg. TOMATOES, seeded and diced

Stir cheese spread and soup together until creamy. Add onions, chiles and tomatoes and stir.

Makes about 5 cups.

Red Hot Dip

1 can (15 oz.) whole TOMATOES, drained
1 sm. ONION, chopped
1 tsp. ground CHILE POWDER
1 Tbsp. SUGAR
1/4 tsp. dried OREGANO LEAVES, from jar

Place all ingredients in the blender. Blend until almost smooth.

Makes about 2 cups.

Pickled Jalapeño Dip

1 pkg. (8 oz.) CREAM CHEESE, softened
1/4 jar (10 oz.) PICKLED JALAPEÑO CHILES, drained
1 jar (2 oz.) diced PIMENTOS, drained
1 can (4 oz.) chopped BLACK OLIVES

Place cream cheese in a medium bowl and stir until creamed. Seed jalapeños, chop and add to cream cheese. Stir well. Add pimentos and olives and stir again.

Makes about 1 1/4 cups.

Cheesy Dip

2 cups processed CHEESE, such as Velveeta®
4 EGGS, hard boiled
1 can (7 oz.) diced GREEN CHILES
1 jar (2 oz.) diced PIMENTOS, drained

Melt cheese in a medium saucepan. Mash eggs in a small bowl and add to melted cheese. Stir in chiles and pimentos. Place in a medium bowl, cover and refrigerate for 48 hours to blend the flavors. Warm to desired dipping consistency.

Makes about 2 1/2 cups.

Jalapeño Piñon Dip

1 pkg. (8 oz.) CREAM CHEESE, softened
1 1/2 Tbsp. JALAPEÑO CHILE, seeded and diced
1 Tbsp. LIME JUICE
1 tsp. CHILI POWDER (or fresh ground CHILE
    POWDER, if available)
1/4 tsp. ground CUMIN
1/2 cup PIÑON NUTS

Soften cream cheese in a medium bowl. Set aside. Place remaining ingredients in a food processor and process until almost smooth. Add to softened cream cheese and blend well. Cover and refrigerate for several hours or overnight.

Makes about 1 1/2 cups.

Mucho Caliente Dip

6 fresh JALAPEÑOS, seeded and finely diced
1 can (15 oz.) TOMATOES, drained and chopped
3 cans (8 oz. each) TOMATO SAUCE
1 tsp. ground CUMIN
1/8 tsp. GARLIC SALT

Combine all ingredients in a medium saucepan. Cook over medium heat for 30 minutes, stirring frequently. Cook mixture and place in a blender. Blend until smooth.

Makes about 4 1/2 cups.

To seed tomatoes, cut them crosswise and scoop seeds out with a spoon.

Green & Red Dip

1 cup SOUR CREAM
1 pkg. (3 oz.) CREAM CHEESE WITH CHIVES, softened
1 can (7 oz.) diced GREEN CHILES, drained
1 lg. or 2 med. TOMATOES, diced
1 can (4 oz.) chopped BLACK OLIVES
4 GREEN ONIONS, chopped

Blend all of the ingredients together. Serve chilled.

Makes about 3 cups.

Mariachi Salsa Dip

2 cups creamed COTTAGE CHEESE
1 cup SALSA

Drain cottage cheese in colander. Place in a small bowl and stir in salsa. Mix well.

Makes about 2 1/2 cups.

Devil's Delight

2 cups COTTAGE CHEESE
1 sm. JALAPEÑO CHILE, peeled and seeded, diced
1/2 cup MAYONNAISE
3 GREEN ONIONS, diced
1 med. TOMATO, diced
2 Tbsp. prepared SALSA

Drain cottage cheese if watery. Combine all ingredients in a medium bowl and chill for 1 hour.

Makes about 2 1/2 cups.

Tomatoes come in three basic shapes: the standard round tomato, small cherry tomatoes and the plum shaped, or Italian, tomato.

Chile Today

1 pkg. (8 oz.) CREAM CHEESE, plain, pimento or chive
1 can (4 oz.) diced GREEN CHILES or
    1 can (4 oz.) PICKLED JALAPEÑO CHILES

Soften cream cheese in a small bowl and stir in chiles of choice. Use green chiles for a mild dip or jalapeño chiles for a hot dip or any combination of chiles that suits your taste.

Makes about 1 cup.

Note: This can also be used as a sandwich spread.

Party Hardy Dip

3 pkgs. (3 oz. each) CREAM CHEESE WITH CHIVES
1 can (4 oz.) diced GREEN CHILES
1 Tbsp. SWEET (white) ONION, minced
1/2 cup medium TACO SAUCE
1/2 tsp. ground CUMIN

Let cream cheese soften in a large bowl. Add remaining ingredients and stir until completely blended.

Makes about 1 1/2 cups.

Hot Stuff

1 cup SOUR CREAM
3/4 cup SALSA
1 jar (2 oz.) PIMENTOS, diced

Combine all the ingredients in a small bowl. Serve chilled.

Makes about 2 cups.

'Atsa Spicy Dip

2 cups SOUR CREAM
1 can (4 oz.) diced GREEN CHILES
1 envelope SPAGHETTI SAUCE MIX

Combine the ingredients in a medium bowl and stir well. Cover bowl and refrigerate several hours or overnight to blend the flavors.

Makes about 2 1/2 cups.

Salsas

Fast & Fresh Salsa

2 med. TOMATOES, chopped
1/3 cup ONION, diced
1 Tbsp. LIME or LEMON JUICE
3 Tbsp. CILANTRO, chopped
1 Tbsp. diced JALAPEÑOS, or to taste

Mix all together and refrigerate.

Makes about 1 cup.

Ranch Salsa

4 med. TOMATOES, chopped
1 can (4 oz.) diced GREEN CHILES, drained
2 GARLIC CLOVES, crushed
1 Tbsp. OLIVE OIL
1 Tbsp. SWEET CIDER VINEGAR
1/2 cup fresh CILANTRO, chopped

Combine in a medium bowl and chill.

Makes about 2 cups.

Salsa means "sauce" in Spanish and is one of the most popular and versatile dishes found anywhere

All Canned Salsa

1 can (15 oz.) whole TOMATOES, drained and chopped
1 can (8 oz.) TOMATO SAUCE
1 can (4 oz.) diced GREEN CHILES, drained
1 Tbsp. dried crushed RED PEPPERS
2 GARLIC CLOVES, crushed
1 Tbsp. dried CILANTRO
1 tsp. RED WINE VINEGAR

Combine all the ingredients and refrigerate. This salsa stores well in the refrigerator and can be frozen.

Makes about 3 cups.

Salsa for a Crowd

3 cans (28 oz. each) stewed TOMATOES, drained
1 can (15 oz.) TOMATO SAUCE
3 med. fresh TOMATOES, diced
3 bunches GREEN ONIONS, chopped
1 Tbsp. canned and chopped JALAPEÑOS
2 GARLIC CLOVES, crushed
1 bunch fresh CILANTRO, chopped
1 can (7 oz.) diced GREEN CHILES
1 tsp. SUGAR

Combine all the ingredients well in a large bowl. Store in glass jars in the refrigerator for up to a week.

Makes about 6 cups.

Heated Dips

Swiss Dip

4 cups SWISS CHEESE, shredded
3 Tbsp. FLOUR
3 cups dry WHITE WINE
1/3 tsp. DRY MUSTARD
ground NUTMEG to taste
2 Tbsp. KIRSCH or BRANDY

In a medium bowl, mix cheese with flour, set aside. Place wine in a deep microwave dish and microwave on high just until wine begins to bubble. Remove from microwave oven and stir in cheese, a small amount at a time, stirring well after each addition, until all the cheese is used and cheese is soft. Return the mixture to the microwave and cook on high for 2-3 minutes or until mixture is thickened and bubbling. Stir in mustard, nutmeg and kirsch or brandy. Serve warm.

Makes about 4 cups.

Nogales Cheese Dip

1 box (1 lb.) VELVEETA® CHEESE, cubed
4 EGGS, hard boiled, chopped
1 can (7 oz.) diced GREEN CHILES

Melt cheese in a microwave safe dish. Add eggs and chiles and stir well. Cool, cover and refrigerate for 2 days to improve flavor. Warm in microwave when ready to serve.

Makes about 3 cups.

Pronto Chili Cheese Dip

1 can (15 oz.) CHILI, any brand
**1 jar (8 oz.) VELVEETA® CHEESE WHIZ, with or
  without jalapeños**

Place chili in a food processor and process until smooth. Place in a small bowl and stir in cheese, blending thoroughly. Serve warm or at room temperature.

Note: In a hurry for a quick supper, this dip can be spread on flour tortillas for a simple burrito.

Quick Mexi-Dip

1 box (1 lb.) Mexican style VELVEETA® CHEESE
1 can (10 oz.) TOMATOES AND GREEN CHILES

Cut cheese into cubes and place in a microwave safe bowl. Add tomatoes and green chiles and stir. Cook on medium power for 10 minutes or until cheese is melted. Stir and serve warm.

Makes about 3 1/2 cups.

Sausage & Cheese Dip

1 pkg. (1 lb.) JIMMY DEAN® SAUSAGE
1 pkg. (1 lb.) Mexican style VELVEETA® CHEESE
1 can (15 oz.) TOMATOES, drained and chopped

Cook sausage in a medium skillet until thoroughly done. Drain well. Melt cheese in microwave or in a medium skillet. When melted, add sausage and tomatoes. Stir well. Serve warm.

Makes about 3 1/2 cups.

Note: Mexican style sausage, called chorizo, can be substituted for the Jimmy Dean sausage.

Chile con Queso

1/2 cup OLIVE OIL
1/2 cup ONIONS, chopped
1 GARLIC CLOVE, crushed
1 JALAPEÑO CHILE, seeded and diced, or 1 can (7 oz.)
    diced GREEN CHILES
1 can (3 oz.) TOMATO PASTE
1 can (28 oz.) TOMATOES, drained
1 can (15 oz.) TOMATOES AND GREEN CHILES, drained
2 cups LONGHORN or MEDIUM CHEDDAR
    CHEESE, grated

Heat olive oil in a large skillet. Sauté onions and garlic until the onions are lightly browned. Add the remaining ingredients, except the cheese, and simmer, uncovered, until medium thick. Cut cheese into small pieces and add to mixture. Simmer until ropy.

Makes about 5 cups.

Cheesy Pecan Dip

1 lb. (4 cups) MEDIUM CHEDDAR CHEESE, grated
1/4 cup ONION, diced
1 tsp. dried RED PEPPERS, crushed, from jar
1 cup MAYONNAISE (not salad dressing)
1 cup PECANS, diced

Combine all the ingredients in a medium bowl and blend well. Serve at room temperature.

Makes about 3 cups.

Che-Broom!
(Cheese, Broccoli & Mushroom Dip)

1 pkg. (10 1/2 oz.) frozen chopped BROCCOLI
1/2 can CREAM OF MUSHROOM SOUP
2 pkgs. (3 oz. each) CREAM CHEESE WITH CHIVES
1 can (8 oz.) MUSHROOMS, diced

Cook broccoli according to package directions, drain well and allow to cool. Place soup, cheese and mushrooms in a medium bowl. Add broccoli and stir. Serve warm or at room temperature.

Makes about 3 cups.

Broccoli Cheese Dip

1 pkg. (10 oz.) frozen chopped BROCCOLI,
   cooked and drained
3 Tbsp. BUTTER or MARGARINE
1/3 cup ONION, chopped
3/4 cup MEDIUM CHEDDAR CHEESE, grated
1 can (10 1/2 oz.) CREAM OF MUSHROOM SOUP
1 can (8 oz.) MUSHROOMS, sliced

    Cook broccoli, set aside. Melt butter or margarine in a medium skillet, add onion and sauté until limp. Add cheese, soup and mushrooms. Stir in broccoli. Mix well and simmer slowly until heated. Do not allow to come to a boil as the cheese will become ropy.

    Makes about 4 1/2 cups.

When cooking fresh broccoli, peel the stems. This allows the tougher stems to cook in the same time as the flowerets.

Drunken Queso Dip

1 cup MEDIUM CHEDDAR CHEESE, finely grated
1 cup JACK CHEESE, finely grated
1/2 cup MAYONNAISE (not salad dressing)
1/8 cup sour mash BOURBON
1/4 tsp. TABASCO® SAUCE
1/2 cup PECANS, crushed

    Place all ingredients in a food processor and blend until smooth. This is best served at room temperature.

    Makes about 2 cups.

Quick Chile con Queso

1 pkg. (8 oz.) Mexican style VELVEETA® CHEESE
1 can (4 oz.) diced GREEN CHILES, drained
dash of ONION SALT

Cube cheese and place in medium microwave safe bowl. Melt in microwave. When cheese is melted, stir in chiles and onion salt.

Makes about 2 cups.

Sonoran Style Dip

2 Tbsp. OLIVE OIL
1 med. ONION, diced
1 can (7 oz.) diced GREEN CHILES
1 cup LONGHORN or MEDIUM CHEDDAR CHEESE, grated
1 cup TOMATOES, peeled, seeded and diced
1/2 cup WHIPPING CREAM

Sauté onions in olive oil in a medium skillet until limp but not browned. Reduce heat to lowest setting and add the remaining ingredients. Stir until warm and the cheese is melted. Serve in a fondue pot.

Makes about 2 cups.

Note: This is also delicious served as a sauce for vegetables and fish.

Velvety Fondue

1 box (1 lb.) Mexican style VELVEETA® CHEESE
6 GREEN ONIONS, diced
1 jar (4 oz.) diced PIMENTOS

Melt cheese in a fondue pot or small saucepan over very low heat. Stir in onions and pimentos. Serve warm.

Makes about 2 cups.

Chorizo Cheese Dip

1 pkg. (12 oz.) CHORIZO (Mexican sausage)
1 lb. Mexican style VELVEETA® CHEESE
1 can (14 1/2 oz.) TOMATOES, drained and chopped

Sauté chorizo in a medium skillet until thoroughly cooked. Drain well and set aside. Melt cheese in a medium bowl in microwave. When cheese is melted, add chorizo and tomatoes.

Makes about 4 cups.

Lentil Dip

1 can (19-20 oz.) LENTIL SOUP
1/4 cup seasoned BREAD CRUMBS
1/4 cup ONION, diced
2 Tbsp. PARSLEY, chopped
1 Tbsp. WHITE WINE VINEGAR

Combine soup and bread crumbs in a medium saucepan. Bring to a gentle boil and simmer and stir for 60 seconds. Remove from heat and stir in the remaining ingredients. Serve warm.

Makes about 2 cups.

Clam It Up Dip

1 stack pkg. RITZ® CRACKERS, crushed (there are
**   4 stack pkgs. in each box of crackers)**
1/2 cup BUTTER or MARGARINE, melted
1/2 tsp. LEMON JUICE
1 can (5 oz.) CLAMS, minced, with liquid
2 Tbsp. ONION, diced

Crush crackers in blender or food processor. In a medium skillet, melt butter or margarine. Add crushed crackers, juice, clams and onion and sauté until onions are limp. Place mixture in a buttered baking dish. Bake in a 350 degree oven for about 30 minutes. Serve warm.

Makes about 2 cups.

Black-eyed Pea Dip

**2 cans (15 oz. each) BLACK-EYED PEAS, with or without
  JALAPEÑOS, drained**
1/4 cup ONION, chopped
1 lg. or 2 sm. GARLIC CLOVES, crushed
1 can (7 oz.) diced GREEN CHILES
1 cup MEDIUM CHEDDAR CHEESE, grated

In a large bowl, mash black-eyed peas. Stir in remaining ingredients. Serve warm.

Makes about 4 cups.

Chile-'Choke Dip

**1 can (15 oz.) ARTICHOKE HEARTS (not marinated),
  drained and chopped**
1 cup MAYONNAISE
1 can (7 oz.) diced GREEN CHILES
1 cup freshly grated PARMESAN CHEESE

Combine the ingredients in a microwave safe dish. Microwave on high for about 3 minutes, rotating the dish once. Serve warm.

Makes about 2 1/2 cups.

Baked Artichoke Dip

1 can (14 oz.) ARTICHOKES, not marinated
1 1/2 cup MAYONNAISE
1 1/2 cup grated PARMESAN CHEESE

In a large bowl, mash artichokes with a fork. Add mayonnaise and cheese. Spread the mixture in a small baking pan and bake in a 350 degree oven for 20-30 minutes or until top is slightly browned. Serve warm or at room temperature.

Makes about 3 1/2 cups.

Hot Artichoke Dip

2 jars (6 oz. each) marinated ARTICHOKE HEARTS,
**   drained and diced**
3/4 cup SOUR CREAM
1/4 cup MAYONNAISE
1/4 cup PARMESAN CHEESE, grated
1 Tbsp. dried TARRAGON LEAVES (from jar)

Combine all ingredients in a medium saucepan and cook over very low heat for approximately 30 minutes. Transfer to a medium serving bowl and serve warm.

Microwave Artichoke Dip

1 lg. can (15 oz.) ARTICHOKE HEARTS,
**   drained and diced**
1 cup MAYONNAISE
1 cup freshly grated PARMESAN CHEESE

Place the ingredients in a microwave dish and stir to mix. Microwave on medium for 5 minutes or until hot and bubbly.

Makes about 2 1/2 cups.

Dessert Dips

Fruity Dip

2 cups COTTAGE CHEESE, well drained
1 carton (8 oz.) CREAM CHEESE WITH
**   STRAWBERRIES, softened**
1 tsp. LEMON JUICE
1 cup STRAWBERRIES, hulled, fresh or frozen

In a medium bowl, cream cottage cheese and cream cheese together until thoroughly blended and smooth. Stir in lemon juice and strawberries.

Makes about 3 1/3 cups.

Note: This dip can be made with a variety of fruits. Use plain cream cheese and add fresh or canned fruits of choice.

Sweetheart Dip

2 pkgs. (8 oz. each) CREAM CHEESE, softened
1 cup PINEAPPLE PRESERVES
1/2 cup mild JALAPEÑO JELLY

Beat all together. Cover and refrigerate at least 24 hours.

Makes about 3 cups.

Walnutty Dip

2 pkgs. (8 oz. each) CREAM CHEESE, softened
1/4 cup POWDERED SUGAR
1 cup WALNUTS, diced
1/4 cup PORT or DUBONNET

Stir cream cheese in a large bowl to soften. Beat in powdered sugar. When thoroughly blended, stir in walnuts and port or Dubonnet. Chill several hours or overnight.

Makes about 2 1/4 cups.

Healthy Dip

2 cups cream style COTTAGE CHEESE
2/3 cup PECANS, finely diced
1/4 cup RAISINS
1/4 cup DATES, chopped
1/4 tsp. ground CINNAMON

Drain cottage cheese, if watery. Place in a medium bowl. Stir in the remaining ingredients.

Makes about 3 cups.

Almond Dip

1 cup plain YOGURT
1 pkg. (8 oz.) ALMOND PIECES
1 Tbsp. LEMON JUICE
1 1/2 tsp. SUGAR
1 tsp. ground GINGER

Place yogurt and almond pieces in a food processor or blender and process until smooth. Add remaining ingredients and blend. Chill well.

Makes 1 cup.

In recipes calling for lemon juice, one-half the amount of vinegar can be used as a substitute.

Tutti-Fruiti Dip

2 cups FRUIT, such as bananas, strawberries or canned
    mixed fruit, drained
1 cup COTTAGE CHEESE, drained
1 pkg. (3 oz.) CREAM CHEESE, softened
1 Tbsp. CINNAMON SUGAR

Combine all the ingredients in a food processor or blender. Process until smooth. Serve well chilled.

Makes about 3 cups.

Aloha Pineapple Dip

2 pkgs. (8 oz. each) CREAM CHEESE, softened
1 lg. can (8 oz.) crushed PINEAPPLE, well drained
1/2 cup YELLOW BELL PEPPER, seeded and finely
    diced
1 cup PECANS, minced

    Soften cream cheese in a medium bowl. Stir in the remaining ingredients. Serve chilled or at room temperature.

    Makes about 2 1/2 cups.

Sweet Dessert Dip

1 carton (15 oz.) RICOTTA or COTTAGE CHEESE
3 Tbsp. SUGAR
2 tsp. VANILLA EXTRACT
1 tsp. grated LEMON PEEL (from jar)
1/2 tsp. ground CINNAMON

    Combine all ingredients in a food processor or blender and blend until smooth. Refrigerate until chilled.

    Makes about 2 cups.

Index

D - G
Dessert Dips

H
Heated Dips

About the Author

Susan K. Bollin is a geologist and an author. She has written extensively in the fields of earth science and environmental science for both adults and children. In addition, she has written books for dog, cat and horse owners. Most recently, Ms. Bollin has written cook books about southwestern and Mexican foods. In addition to *Chip and Dip Lovers Cook Book,* she is also the author of *Salsa Lovers Cook Book, Quick-n-Easy Mexican Recipes* and *Sedona Cook Book.* She and her family live in Arizona.

QUICK-N-EASY
MEXICAN RECIPES

More than 175 favorite Mexican recipes you can prepare in less than thirty minutes. Traditional items such as tacos, tostadas and enchiladas. Also features easy recipes for salads, soups, breads, desserts and drinks. **By Susan K. Bollin.**

5 1/2 x 8 1/2—128 pages . . . $5.95

SALSA LOVERS COOK BOOK

More than 180 taste-tempting recipes for salsas that will make every meal a special event! Salsas for salads, appetizers, main dishes, and desserts! Put some salsa in your life! **By Susan K. Bollin.**

5 1/2 x 8 1/2—128 pages . . . $5.95

SEDONA COOK BOOK
Recipes from Red Rock Country

Mouth-watering recipes inspired by the beauty of Sedona and its awesome landscape guarantee an extraordinary culinary experience. Recipes like *Sinagua Steaks, Copper Cliffs Coleslaw, Camp Verde Gazpacho* and *Castle Rock Rum Balls* to tease your palate. Includes fascinating Sedona trivia! **By Susan K. Bollin.**

5 1/2 x 8 1/2—120 pages . . . $7.95